For all my loved ones who have given me a home:
my parents, F&S, M&A—CL

For my parents, Kang & Song—PK

Library of Congress Cataloging-in-Publication data is on file with the publisher.
Text copyright © 2021 by Carol Lawrence
Illustrations copyright © 2021 by Albert Whitman & Company
Illustrations by Poppy Kang
First published in the United States of America in 2021
by Albert Whitman & Company

ISBN 978-0-8075-3365-9 (hardcover)
ISBN 978-0-8075-3364-2 (ebook)

Printed in China

10 9 8 7 6 5 4 3 2 1 WKT 24 23 22 21 20

Design by Rick DeMonico

For more information about Albert Whitman & Company,
visit our website at www.albertwhitman.com

No matter what they are like or when they were built, homes have always been very important. They give us shelter from weather, safety from predators, and help us feel secure. We build houses in which to make our homes.

Houses are built from many different materials. The way they were made used to depend on what was available—wood from forests or granite mined from rocks. There wasn't a big choice. As technology advanced, so did our homes. Building materials could be shipped around the world. Now, there is concrete, steel, and glass. From homes of one story, people can now build up.

The environment just outside a home affects what building materials can be used, and the climate affects the way a home is built. Hurricanes and tornadoes mean that homes have to be able to stand up to strong winds and heavy rains. If people live in an earthquake area, they limit the height of their homes and make sure that homes can sway in strong shaking. Homes in hot climates have to block strong sunlight and heat.

From fires that give off a warm glow to boilers that provide central heating; from candles and oil-filled lanterns to electricity that gives us light at the flick of a switch; from chamber pots kept underneath beds to outhouses to indoor plumbing—health and safety standards have changed both the kinds of homes we live in and the way we live.

One of the biggest influences on homes is the culture of the people who live in them. Cultural changes in society make a big difference to where people choose to live and the homes in which we live. Outside influences such as war and technology change society, so they change the ways we live and our homes.

For as far back as there are records, people have always wanted some kind of home. Our earliest ancestors slept in caves, convenient, ready-made homes. Cave dwellers only had to find one that offered shelter, and they could move right in. But cave people didn't just stay in caves all day and night; they spent much of their time outdoors, hunting for food.

They hunted animals such as mammoths and bison, which migrated throughout the year in search of food. When on the move, cave people followed the animals, learning to make tents from animal skins that could be packed up and taken along. Cave homes gave shelter, safety, and security, even if they were temporary.

Cave people lived at least 200,000 years ago. The Neanderthals, whose limestone caves were well preserved, lived in Eurasia from the Atlantic regions of Europe eastward to central Asia. At the same time, people also lived in eastern Asia and in Africa.

Ancestors of contemporary Native Americans were nomadic hunter-gatherers. They moved in small family groups from Asia to North America during the last Ice Age, from about 30,000 to 12,000 years ago, walking across a land bridge between Asia and North America that was exposed in low sea levels. These Paleo-Indians, as they are now called, used fire and had domesticated dogs, but did not use the wheel. They hunted woolly mammoths, giant ground sloths, and large bison.

Native people lived in different parts of America and homes differed from region to region. The Navajo in the Southwest used adobe, a mix of straw, mud, and sand, to build their pueblos.

People who lived in pueblos added rooms on top of existing ones as they were needed. A house could have many levels.

Wickiups were made of arched poles covered with mats and brush.

Tribes of the California mountains built circular homes called wickiups. They were short-term homes, taken down as the inhabitants moved around to hunt.

Native tribes near the northwest coast lived in rectangular lodges. Several families lived in one house and cooked on a fire pit in the center.

Lodges had wood frames covered by planks of wood from nearby forests.

The northwest coast tribes were known for their artistic totem poles outside their lodges. Totem poles were wooden carvings with symbols of figures to honor their ancestors, events, people, or animals.

Some Native people of the Great Plains hunted and followed buffalo herds. They built teepees from long wooden poles cut from trees, which they covered with animal skins, and collapsed to carry with them.

Teepee poles were tied together at the top and spread out to make a circle at the bottom. The skins were often painted with powdered pigment colors on the outside.

The igloo is a temporary, dome-shaped winter home usually built from blocks of ice or snow by the Inuit in one large area in the Northwest Territories of Canada. In summer, the Inuit now live in cloth tents. The Inuit used to put large dishes filled with animal oil in the centers of the igloos, which they burned like candles.

The Inuit built their igloos with blocks of ice.

Native tribes in the Eastern woodlands built rectangular longhouses with a barrel-shaped roof and rooms for families on both sides of a long hallway. People slept on low platforms. High platforms held supplies.

Longhouses were wooden frames covered with strips of bark from woodland trees, sewn together.

Native tribes of the Northeast also used trees and bark from nearby forests to build wigwams. Even though the homes were small, sometimes more than one family lived in them.

Wigwams were made from poles from trees, bent into a dome-shape, tied, and covered with bark.

Southeastern tribes built a chickee, with a thatched roof to keep off the rain and open sides to keep the inside cool.

The Dutch, Germans, French, and Spanish came to America before the British, and built homes like those they'd left behind. The Spanish settled in what they called the New World in the 1400s and, like the Navajo before them, used adobe covered with white stucco to build thick-walled colonial homes in the South, West, and Southwest.

Spanish colonial homes had red barrel roof tiles.

Walls were thick to keep out the sun's heat.

The adobe was made from sun-dried bricks cemented with mud.

There were long, narrow porches on the outside, instead of hallways.

Many contemporary American homes are based on homes built in early Britain; the British brought their ideas of houses when they first built settlements in America in 1607, with changes for available materials and climate. Early British homes were built from wood, with large stone chimneys.

Colonial-style homes were rectangular and symmetrical. These homes were popular in the 1700s, before the American Revolution, which lasted from 1775 to 1783. Most homes had two or three rooms, but the wealthy lived in mansions that had a central opening onto four square rooms.

The homes were brick with one large chimney in the middle or two smaller ones at either end.

The front windows were lined up in rows and columns.

After the War of Independence, American settlers started building different kinds of homes from those they'd left behind.
The first homes in America after the Revolution ended in 1783 were small, one-room houses. Life wasn't about comfort; it was about growing and finding food.

Roofs were usually thatched.

A fireplace was for cooking food and for heat.

Furniture might have been only a table, a bench, a bed, and a chest for clothing.

Floors were dirt, and windows were holes in the walls covered with paper.

Many homes were wooden frames filled in with sticks covered with mud and grass.

But as the colonies grew, the wealthy landowners in the South made the African people they enslaved build plantations, which were large farms with larger houses than those of the northern settlers. The styles of the homes still often reflected where the settlers were from: Germany, the Netherlands, Spain, and Britain.

Homes in cities were smaller than plantations, but with wooden floors and paneled walls. They were two or three stories tall, and well furnished, with sofas and chairs, rugs, and big beds that had comfortable feather mattresses.

No matter how comfortable homes were, they didn't have electricity or running water. Rugs may have been on floors, but they were also on walls to keep drafts out. Sometimes, older children slept in attics, which weren't insulated against the cold.

As settlers moved west, they built log cabins if there were trees nearby; log cabins were easy and quick to construct. Most log cabins were one room where the whole family lived. If the settlers stayed, they built larger homes or added to the original cabin.

Windows were holes cut in the logs, covered with greased paper.

A stone fireplace was built at one end of the cabin, to cook food and to help warm the home.

Cracks between the logs were filled in with mud or clay.

The cabins were built by cutting notches into the logs at each end, so they slotted together closely.

Doors usually faced south, so the sun could shine in during the day.

Each side of the cabin was about 15 feet long.

Homes in the late 1700s and early 1800s were built in what is called a Federal, or Adam, style.

Houses were still built with available materials so, in the Northeast, homes were made with clapboard, while in the South and cities in the North, they were brick, to help with fireproofing.

Houses were a simple square or rectangle, two or three stories high, with two rooms on each floor.

Roofs had triangular gables at the front.

Sash windows were lined up in rows and columns and had small panes, six at the top and six at the bottom.

Rooms often had simple curved walls and arches above interior doors.

The outside of the house was more decorative than the interior. There might have been a small porch with fancy moldings, and narrow, simple columns.

At around this time, there was a huge cultural shift in the United States and around the world, one that changed society forever: the First Industrial Revolution, which started in Britain in the mid-1760s and reached North America as the Second Industrial Revolution in the late 1800s. The steam engine had been invented in 1698 and improved a few times until finally, in 1778, mechanical work was powered by steam.

The steam engine led to railroads, and to the steamboat, which led to passenger ships crossing the country by canal. Before the Industrial Revolution, many factories were powered by water, so they had to be near a river. Now, factories could be anywhere.

From the time that the United States was founded in 1776, manufacturing had been done locally, in small shops. But now, manufacturing was being done in large factories, in big cities. Many people left the small towns and moved to cities. Many families were now split up, living in different parts of the country.

People needed to live near the factories, and they needed homes that weren't expensive. Many houses were built in terraced rows; not all of them were built well. The United States now had slums of small houses where the working classes lived—too many people in too small an area. The houses had shared toilets and were damp. Eventually, health and safety regulations improved the lives of workers.

There was a growing middle class, too, living in well-built, well-furnished homes with clean running water. The economy of the country was changing along with the houses.

With better transportation, building materials could be moved more quickly around the country. People no longer had to rely on what was available nearby. From a rural, farming society, the United States changed to an urban, manufacturing one. The country was building, growing, fast. The whole world was changing.

Houses in the North were built with wooden frames and brick, and houses in the West were now being made from sod instead of log cabins, but some houses in the South, where much of the Civil War was fought, remained on farming plantations. The invention of the cotton gin replaced hand labor with machines that separated the cotton seeds from the fiber. Plantations were doing well financially because of this change to machine work.

Using the free labor of the people they enslaved, some plantation owners built grand, elegant, large houses. Almost all the buildings on plantations were built from local resources, including the bricks and stone, along with the wood.

Most of the enslaved people, though, who picked the cotton, had to live in slave quarters, set apart from the main houses. These small, basic houses, built for sleeping, not living, were usually only one room and one story, with few or no comforts. Floors were dirt or raised for air to circulate. Enslaved people who worked in the main house instead of in the fields either lived in the main house or had their own homes.

Between the end of the Civil War in 1865 and the start of World War I in 1914, the population of the United States grew quickly. More than twenty-five million immigrants came from all over the world. The telephone was invented; so was the electric light. Society kept changing.

It changed even more after 1914. Cities grew, so more homes, many of them apartment buildings, were built. Enslaved people were freed but were not treated as equal to white people. A change was made to the Constitution of the United States that made it illegal for people to be denied the right to vote because of their sex; this meant that many women could vote. Cross-country railroads were built. Some Native people began living the way settlers did but many fought to live according to their customs. Farming boomed because of all the immigrants and because transporting produce was now easier. Large farmhouses held large families. Businesses formed corporations. The United States was now the world's leading industrial nation. World War I kept the factories busy, with women taking over from men at war overseas.

After World War I ended in 1918, the American middle class kept growing, so more houses were built. But the Great Depression, which began in 1929, slowed growth until around 1939 when World War II began. During those years, people lost their jobs and homes. Men and women joined the military and those who stayed home were recruited to work in factories.

The years after World War II ended in 1945 were a time of growth, success, and optimism in the United States. Men back from war bought their own homes and farms. Families wanted settled lives. The suburb was born in the 1950s, with a housing boom for the new middle class. Low-income people lived in government-led housing across the country; their lives were not as comfortable as the rising middle class.

Suburbs near cities were residential so men could commute by train and car. The mass-produced houses, called cookie-cutter, were alike, built for a mother who stayed home, a father who went to work, and two children.

Men who had become wealthy after the war built new homes that were larger and more individual, with more bedrooms and land. Some wealthy people moved back into cities, so apartments became bigger and more luxurious. Poorer people still struggled financially, and lived in small houses and cramped apartments across the country, some in slums.

Typical homes had three bedrooms, a kitchen with modern appliances, and a table where the family ate; there was often a garage for the car, and a small plot of land that included a back yard.

Apartment houses today are usually made from concrete, reinforced with steel girders. They have central heating and air-conditioning. There are elevators.

Some buildings are now more than one hundred stories high, looking down on the clouds. People want to live close to where they work and there wouldn't be space for enough private houses. Most things that people need are in the buildings where they live because people value time, and anything that gives them more time is considered good.

Smart apartments also give people more time. There are smart lights that turn themselves on and off, smart locks, smart thermostats, and smart blinds. Smart apartments are wired to cell phones, computers, washing machines and dryers, dishwashers—even pets' feeding stations. Smart homes are meant to give people easier lives.

Our homes continue to give us shelter, safety, and security, while reflecting our society. The jobs we have, the kinds of relationships we have, the size of our families, the lifestyles we have—all determine how we live. It's always been this way, since the hunter-gatherers. Changes in society mean changes in our homes.

Author's Note

Homes have always been a place for people to shelter, whether it's from the weather or from war. Homes have helped to determine society—our culture and how we interact with one another. And at the same time, the opposite is true: our society has helped to determine the kinds of homes we have. City homes are built for one kind of culture, and they are very different from farmhouses or country homes, which are built for other kinds of culture.

Homes and society have helped shape each other and have grown more sophisticated together. Just as society is constantly changing, so are our homes.

But the need for shelter, safety, and comfort has never changed. This is what a home, no matter what kind it is, represents for people everywhere.

And never have our homes been more important to us than they have been since the beginning of 2020, when our world and almost everything in it became unsafe because of the COVID-19 pandemic. Governments around the world told people to stay home. Home, the one place where most of us are certain to feel, and be, safe.

Glossary

Civil War: in the United States this is also called the War between the States, which took place from 1861–1865.

colonial: of or relating to the time when the United States was made up of the original thirteen colonies.

First and Second Industrial Revolutions: time periods during which the world changed from farming to machine production.

Great Depression: a time during much of the 1930s when business and employment around the world stopped growing and it was difficult to find work.

Ice Age: a time between 35,000–120,000 years ago when much of the world was covered in ice.

prehistoric: of or relating to the time before written records.

rural: of or relating to the countryside.

urban: of or relating to a town or city.

World War I: the war from 1914–1918 in which countries around the world chose sides and fought one another.

World War II: the war from 1939–1945 in which countries around the world chose sides and fought one another.